What people are saying about

Practical Mystics

Jennifer Kavanagh has written a lovely book which I found to be compelling reading. In a very practical way she explains the meaning of mysticism for Quakers and how an experience, which some might regard as being esoteric, can be truly meaningful for many today.
Terry Waite

This is a delightful book, blending the author's personal experience with a really helpful overview of the nature of mysticism. It is clearly written, very accessible, but above all inspiring. *Practical Mystics* encourages each of us to live into that role.
Ben Pink Dandelion, Woodbrooke Quaker Study Centre

Jennifer Kavanagh has done us a great service in writing a book that pinpoints one of the most elusive and intangible elements of Quaker life. *Practical Mystics* is about the subtle balance between spiritual experience and the action it brings about, between the stillness of a Quaker meeting and the clamour of the world. How does the mystical become the practical? Is there a transition point? Why do they merge? She answers these questions with thoughtfulness, insight and wisdom, writing as vividly about spiritual inwardness as she does about the urgent, unstoppable impulse to give service to others. The result is an inspiring book about a wellspring of inspiration. I thoroughly recommend it.
Geoffrey Durham, author of *The Spirit of the Quakers* and *Being a Quaker: a guide for newcomers*

Jennifer is one of the most interesting writers of our generation on spirituality.

Derek A. Collins, London Centre for Spirituality

In *Practical Mystics*, Jennifer Kavanagh introduces readers to the genius of the Quaker way – spirituality experienced in the midst of day-to-day life thus empowering those who try it to live deeply and well.

J. Brent Bill, author of *Holy Silence: The Gift of Quaker Spirituality*

QUAKER QUICKS

Practical Mystics
Quaker faith in action

QUAKER QUICKS

Practical Mystics
Quaker faith in action

Jennifer Kavanagh

CHRISTIAN
ALTERNATIVE

Winchester, UK
Washington, USA

JOHN HUNT PUBLISHING

First published by Christian Alternative Books, 2019
Christian Alternative Books is an imprint of John Hunt Publishing Ltd.,
No. 3 East St., Alresford, Hampshire SO24 9EE, UK
office@jhpbooks.com
www.johnhuntpublishing.com
www.christian-alternative.com

For distributor details and how to order please visit the 'Ordering' section on our website.

ISBN: 978 1 78904 279 5
978 1 78904 280 1 (ebook)
Library of Congress Control Number: 2017953307

A CIP catalogue record for this book is available from the British Library.

Design: Stuart Davies

UK: Printed and bound by CPI Group (UK) Ltd, Croydon, CR0 4YY
Printed in North America by CPI GPS partners

We operate a distinctive and ethical publishing philosophy in
all areas of our business, from our global network of authors to
production and worldwide distribution.

Contents

By the same author

The Methuen Book of Animal Tales (ed.)
The Methuen Book of Humorous Stories (ed.)
Call of the Bell Bird
The World is our Cloister
New Light (ed.)
Journey Home (formerly *The O of Home*)
Simplicity Made Easy
Small Change, Big Deal
The Failure of Success
A little book of Unknowing
Heart of Oneness

Fiction
The Emancipation of B
The Silence Diaries

Preface

There are some 400,000 Quakers throughout the world, most of them in Africa. For historical reasons, there are different traditions in different parts of the world. Some are more akin to evangelical churches; some are pastor-led. Although all Quakers have much in common, I can only write about my own tradition, the unprogrammed liberal wing that is to be found in the UK, Europe, some parts of the US, South Africa, Australia and New Zealand.

And, though there will be references to the events and attitudes of former times and how things have changed, I will also be concentrating on present-day Quakers. There are enough misconceptions about Quakers based on the bonnet-wearers of the past. This is not a book about theology, it is a book about experience: of others and of my own. The experience of seeking and sensing the presence of God, and how it affects how what we do and how we are in the world.

"Quaker" is a nickname given to us by a scornful judge in the seventeenth century – but it's one we are happy to use. The official name for Quakers is the Religious Society of Friends, and we usually call each other "Friend". As the word "Friend" can be ambiguous, I shall generally use the term "Quaker" here, but where the term "Friend" (with a capital "F") appears, that means the same.

References in the text are to the books in Further Reading. Where there is more than one book by an author, the reference in the text gives the date.

Thanks to the many Friends who have shared their experience and knowledge. They include: Frances Crampton, Ben Pink Dandelion, Rob Francis, Harvey Gillman, Chris Goodchild, Maud Grainger, Ben Jarman, John Lampen, Stuart Masters. Any errors are my own.

1

Introduction

I recently heard Quakers described by a priest as "practical mystics". It is a phrase often used about us – and also about at least another two religious groups to my certain knowledge – and I sometimes question whether Friends have any time for it at all. Practical? Perhaps we are. But mystics? I wonder. There is something gloriously no-nonsense about almost all the Quakers I know.

(Quaker Quest, 18)

Yes, Quakers are sometimes called "practical mystics". Why? What does it mean? Is it appropriate?

"Practical mystics" is an odd phrase: seemingly a contradiction in terms. Whether a Christian hermit or a Hindu fakir, a mystic is generally considered to be removed from the world, other-worldly, indeed. But even nuns and monks, hidden behind monastic walls, their lives devoted to God, often lead pretty practical lives, both within and outside their establishments. Managing all the practical affairs of the building and community, running businesses and teaching.

But I shall focus here on people who are living in the world. What I hope to describe is a group who combine mysticism with often radical action. To look not just at how the contemplative and active lives can co-exist but how in essence they are the same. Practical people, all of whom can be mystics; mystics who can also be practical. And, more than that, how the action stems from that very faith, how the two are intertwined, and how crucial that interaction is.

The term seems first to have come into currency in the early part of the twentieth century, notably in the book, *Practical Mysticism*, written by Evelyn Underhill and first published in 1915. The author was committed to contemplation all her

3

life, though, moving between the Church of England and the Catholic Church, she found it hard to find an appropriate religious context. In her book Underhill sets out her belief that spiritual life is part of human nature and as such is available to every human being. For her, the very nature of mysticism itself is practical – a realistic part of human nature.

The writer most known for applying the term "practical mystics" to Quakers was the twentieth-century American Quaker, Rufus Jones. Although a dozen years older than Evelyn Underhill, most of his books on mysticism were published in the 1920s, a few years after the publication of *Practical Mysticism*. The two authors, one in the UK and the other in the US, admired, and on occasion quoted from, each other's work.

* * *

When I came to Quakers, some twenty years ago, I found myself plunged not only into a spiritual quest but also, unexpectedly, into an engagement with the world.

It was in the late 1990s. After the break-up of my marriage and, a few years later, another relationship ended, something strange began to happen to me. I had had no religious faith since I was about eighteen but now, every time I went into a church – to look at the architecture or for a christening – I would find myself in tears. To paraphrase the Franciscan Richard Rohr, transformation was happening, but I did not know it yet. If I'd known, I might have tried to stop it or take charge. Something was going on within me that I did not understand but felt powerless to resist. I had no idea what was happening, but had no choice but to pursue whatever it was. I tried some local churches and ran out. They were not what I was looking for.

I remembered seeing the sign outside the Quaker Meeting House in St Martin's Lane in London, and decided to try it. At the time I didn't think I knew much about the Religious Society of Friends (Quakers) but I later realised that there had been signposts along the way that I hadn't been ready to see.

I don't remember my first Quaker Meeting. What I do remember is that, after a darkly troubled time, I found peace. At first, I spoke to no one. Although I am a sociable person, I didn't want my social self to trample on the shoots of something so new and tender. But I read books from the meeting house library – and couldn't believe what I was reading. It was so different from anything that my previous experience of religion as an Anglican had led me to expect. There was nothing to sign up to, no set words or hymns; the meeting house itself was bare of ornamentation and symbols. Everything external was stripped away, so that the focus could be on the direct experience of God. And it was not a priest or the scriptures that was the ultimate authority but our experience of what the founder of Quakers, George Fox, referred to as the Inward Light shining in our souls.

I had no idea religion could be like this – this was ME! It gave me permission to be myself. More than that, it was a *requirement* to be myself. Not easy, as we know. A lifetime's task. As the weeks went on, I realised that I had come home. Such a discovery is almost a cliché of the spiritual life. In listening to men and women of many faiths, I have heard many talk of "coming home". And that "home" can be somewhere that is found for the first time. What I had found was a response to what had been going on within me. And an invitation to a direct relationship with the Divine.

I discovered that at the heart of the Quaker way is a belief that all human beings have the capacity for a direct relationship with the Divine, and at the core of their practice is the Meeting for Worship, in which those present still themselves in an active waiting on God.

Finding a spiritual home is a complex matter. People come to Quakers for a number of reasons. It may be a dissatisfaction with an existing faith group; it may be to find a context for their faith, an answer to their spiritual seeking. It may be because they have come across Quakers in social action or peace marches, and feel that this is a group that represents their own life values. It may be to find community.

In my own case, I was not looking for a community; I was responding to a restless longing within myself that at the time had no name.

Chapter 1

Mysticism

We cannot say that there is a separate "mystical sense", which some men have and some have not, but rather that every human soul has a certain latent capacity for God, and that in some this capacity is realised with an astonishing richness. Such a realisation may be of many kinds and degrees – personal or impersonal, abrupt and ecstatic, or peaceful and continuous. This will depend partly on the temperament of the mystic, and partly on his religious background and education.

(Underhill, quoted in Jones, 1927: 203)

What is mysticism? It's a word that arouses a lot of confusion and, in some cases, suspicion. According to Wikipedia, it is "the pursuit of communion with, identity with, or conscious awareness of an ultimate reality, divinity, spiritual truth, or God through direct experience, intuition, or insight". The word only entered the English language in the mid-eighteenth century, but "mystic" both as an adjective and as a noun, is far earlier, dating from the late Middle Ages. Part of the Oxford English Dictionary definition (dating from 1637 and now said to be "rare") is: "Pertaining to or connected with the branch of theology which relates to the direct communication of the soul with God".

But our word mysticism comes from the Greek *mystikos*, an initiate of a mystery religion, and the OED definition also refers to something hidden, mysterious, occult, and only for the initiated, which may be the reason for the suspicions which have attended it. And it is true that secrecy has attended many mystic movements over the centuries – either because its adherents felt that such experiences were only for the initiated and might be contaminated by exposure, or from fear of persecution.

And persecution there was. There has always been a tension between institutional religion and those of a mystical tendency, especially in the Christian Church. Those who believe in direct unmediated experience of the Divine are often regarded with suspicion because their different priorities are seen as a challenge to the authority of the Church and, not least, because they are less easy to control. From the eleventh century on, writes Bernard McGinn in his collection of pieces on Christian mysticism, there was:

> a significant growth of popular movements condemned as heretical. Heresies of a mystical nature first appeared in the second half of the thirteenth century, but grew rapidly in the late Middle Ages. These heretics were accused of ... neglect of the sacraments and of ecclesiastical authority, pretensions to a higher knowledge of God, esotericism ... There were growing fears of dangerous mysticism in the late Middle Ages and ... these fears set many of the criteria used in subsequent centuries for the investigation and condemnation of what was seen as mystical heresy. (490)

Among those accused and often persecuted for that heresy were many well-known individual mystics, but also groups such as the Cathars and Rosicrucians. And, in the seventeenth century the Quakers, whose abolition of a paid priesthood and refusal to pay tithes or take oaths challenged the traditions of the Church, paid the price for their refusal to conform. Thousands, including George Fox, founder of the Quakers, were imprisoned and most harshly treated. Until well into the nineteenth century, Quakers and other nonconformists were excluded from university, politics and many areas of public life.

Evelyn Underhill gives a definition of "mysticism" that she feels will suit most purposes. It is one that I am content to use:

Mysticism is the art of union with Reality. The mystic is one who has attained that union in greater or less degree; or who aims at and believes in such attainment.
(1991:2)

In his study and anthology of mysticism F.C. Happold also adopts Underhill's definition, and remarks that it is both "a form of experience and a type of consciousness" (38).

Underhill's use of the word "Reality" is significant. There are many who find the word "God" uncomfortable. Mysticism can be found in people of all religions and none, from both inside and outside the framework of institutional religion. William Blake, William Wordsworth and many other poets demonstrate that a mystic experience can arise from a non-religious setting, especially in the natural world. As one of my friends said: "Is suddenly awakening to the indivisible unity of all things when walking in a wood any different from experiencing Christ in the Eucharist?" Mysticism, in its very nature unconfined by any specific bound of institution or creed, inherently tends to universalism. Many writers affirm this universalist view of mysticism including, more recently, Dorothee Soelle:

Mystical experience is not, then, something extraordinary, requiring some special talent or sixth sense. Thousands of people in other cultures have had such experiences, experiences of this happiness, this wholeness, this sense of being at home in the world, of being at one with God. It makes no difference – and this point has been confirmed by everyone who has ever reported on mystical experience – whether these experiences are interpreted with the aid of a personal God or nontheistically, as in oriental mysticism. Whether we see these experiences in terms of the Tao or of God is not central to them. How we view them will depend on the culture we live in, our past experiences, the languages we have learned.

Many others have come to the same conclusion, and the extensive collection of the Alister Hardy Research Centre reveals an extraordinary wealth of over six thousand accounts of religious and non-religious experiences. In his seminal *The Varieties of Religious Experience* about mystic experience across the faiths (first published in 1902), William James finds, through his extensive research, that the mystic experience is not reliant on a particular religion. James also found that, however different practice and tradition may be in different religions, at the mystic level, religions come together.

The other day I heard Quakers referred to as a "mystical sect of Christianity". Apart from any discomfort with the word "sect", which has a completely misleading connotation of exclusivity, could this be a realistic description of Quakers? It's not how most Quakers would see themselves, feeling that "mystic" is a big word for what they are and do. But what is the mystic experience but a direct experience of God? And however little we achieve it, the intention of Quakers' core practice of Meeting for Worship is just that.

Brought up a Quaker, Rufus Jones felt that mysticism had been a part of his life since early childhood, referring to:

the unnamed and unconscious mystical propensity of my family. The word "mystical" was never spoken and of course had never been heard in our circle. It was implicit practice and not explicit theory that counted. I was immersed in a group mystical life from the very birth of consciousness and memory.
(1940: 40)

Jones calls mysticism "the attitude of mind which comes into correspondence with a spiritual world-order that is felt to be as real as the visible one" (210), and a mystic as someone who has a "vital reciprocal correspondence with God" (*ibid.*, 249).

The important emphasis that Underhill and Jones give is to the experiential nature of mysticism, rather than, as the OED definition has it, a theology. "We are concerned with the experience itself, not with secondhand formulations of it," says Jones (1940: 97), and Soelle concurs:

The crucial point here is that in the mystical understanding of God, experience is more important than doctrine, the inner light more important than church authority, the certainty of God and communication with him more important than believing in his existence or positing his existence rationally.

And the major contribution of these writers was to democratise it. The popular conception of mystics and mystical experience is that it is something exclusive, elite, soaring above the scope of the ordinary person. This is very far from the truth. As Underhill puts it: "The world of Reality exists for all; and all may participate in it, unite with it, according to their measure and to the strength and purity of their desire" (1991:7). According to her, Jones and others, mysticism is not just for the initiated or those with special gifts, but for everyone. After her major work, *Mysticism*, written some years before, Underhill's book *Practical Mysticism* is addressed to "the ordinary man".

The history of mystic experience over the centuries and in all faiths is full of individuals with remarkable experience and powers: they testify to a state of being that few of us will attain, except, perhaps occasionally in what we would term a peak experience. We can marvel at and be inspired by the accounts of such figures as St John of the Cross, Hildegarde of Bingen, Teresa of Avila or Julian of Norwich, whom Happold calls "developed" or "true" mystics, but we don't imagine that we will ascend to such a contemplative state of being. Nonetheless, according to

Happold,

> mystical consciousness is much more common than a capacity to rise to the heights of Contemplation. To more than is supposed, since they seldom talk about it, there has come, even if only dimly, the experience of "the intersection of the timeless moment".
>
> They may not call themselves mystics, but in a lesser degree, they have known something that the true contemplative knows in a more intense and continuous form. (122, 19)

Not only is the popular conception of mysticism that it is something rarified, but also that it is expressed in extreme ways: in trances, in ecstatic experiences; in dramatic physical and spiritual manifestations. This may be true of some mystic experiences, but is far from the generality. We, as individuals, may occasionally have what is termed a peak experience but as I was told by a Buddhist teacher, it is as well not to be attached to them. For as Teresa of Ávila, herself prone to trances and levitations, warned: they are not the bread and butter of the spiritual life.

If we stick to our definition, we will know that our glimpses of an alternative reality do not have to be expressed in such dramatic ways. As Jones says: "The seasoned Quaker in the corporate hush and stillness of a silent meeting is far removed from ecstasy, but he is not the less convinced that he is meeting with God" (98).

And many of us in our daily lives, and more often during worship or meditation, have glimpses, times when we are conscious of a deeper reality, a time when we sense the unity of all creation, when the observer and observed are one.

> In mystical peak experiences it is commonplace to be held in a unity of time and eternity, place and infinity. When we are stilled, present, in the moment, when we allow eternity to

enter our lives, the relentlessness of the clock and of our lives loses its power and we can begin to approach such moments of fruition ... The popular view of contemplatives is that they are absent-minded. The reverse is true. They are present-minded.
(Kavanagh, 138–9)

Spiritual experiences often begin in childhood, when perhaps we are more open to an alternative reality, when it has not been overlaid with conflicting experiences or we have not yet learned to keep them quiet. In my early teens I regularly had out-of-body experiences, looking down on myself from a position floating near the ceiling of the room. I thought such experiences were commonplace; when I learned that they were not, I closed them down.

But the question that might arise is how does anyone know that any religious experience is a connection with God? "What guarantee", asks Jones, "does the mystic possess that he has passed the bounds of space and time and has come upon the transcendent Reality – *That Which Is?*" (1940: 24). In an unpublished pamphlet on "Quaker Mysticism: its context and its implications", the American political scientist Mulford Sibley feels that "the answer is that it is self-evident and that the self-evidence is so powerfully impressed on the transformed consciousness that they cannot doubt it".

In analysing many accounts across the centuries and from different religions, William James found a way of discerning whether an experience is indeed a mystical one. He identified four qualities common to all peak experiences. He found that they are "ineffable" (that is, that they cannot be described), that they are transient, that they are generally passive and that they are "noetic" (i.e. have some content of knowing). On returning to normal sensory reality, the mystic finds himself in an expanded awareness. Everything is changed. Such experiences also bear some sense of unity – a breaking down of divisions and boundaries between the viewer and the viewed. All is one. "In mystic states", James writes, "we both become one with the Absolute and we become aware of our oneness ... There is about mystical utterances an eternal unanimity which ought to make a critic stop and think" (419).

The Quaker Rufus Jones describes the effect of mystical experience as "heightened moral, spiritual, and practical power, released and set into action by a personal experience of God present in their lives" (1940:103).

By far the larger number of mystics probably live and die without explicitly knowing that they *are* mystics ... They practice the presence of God instead of arriving at a clear statement of knowledge about it ... This may well be called practical mysticism ... mysticism of life and action.
(*ibid.*, 106)

In a lovely phrase, Jones says that "they walk about their ordinary tasks of life without knowing that their faces shine" (1927: 203).

Commitment to the contemplative life has, in some cases, led to extremes of isolation and self-denial, sometimes as an expression of expiation for what is seen as sinfulness in the individual and in mankind. Like the Dominican Matthew Fox in his book of the same name, Quakers are more at home with the idea of "original blessing": a sense of celebration of and gratitude for life in all its forms. Wishing to distance himself from any world-denying practices, Jones refers to "affirmation mysticism", expressing the view that God can be intimately experienced in the course of everyday living and that we are fulfilled not negated by the experience.

That is not to deny that in order to access a different dimension there needs to be a degree of surrender, a letting go of the ego, of the need to control, of all that blocks us from God, whether that be excessive busyness, or preoccupation with possessions or status. Yes, Quaker worship has been stripped of external inessentials, but for our attention to be single-minded there needs to be an equivalent simplification of our own lives. To listen to and hear the still small voice, we need to allow space for Spirit. As the French monk and sannyasi Abhishiktananda says: "God dwells only where man steps back to give him room."

Stepping back – that is good. I have always struggled with early mystic accounts of the need to annihilate the self. Harvey Gillman is helpful here:

> It is not the annihilation of the one in order to give way to the other. It is an intimate encounter with the "other", which restores. It is a form of recognition – the limited recognises but cannot define the limitless. (12)

In modern times, although there are mystical strands of many religions, such as the Kabbalists in Judaism and Sufis in Islam, they are regarded more as fringe than mainstream. In contemporary Christianity, although there are strong mystical tendencies in many parts of the church, especially in the Eastern Orthodox and Roman Catholic denominations, there is no such recognised separate mystical group.

Except.

What about the Quakers? And the entirely mystic nature of their Meeting for Worship.

Chapter 2

Meeting for Worship

Friends, meet together and know one another in that which is
eternal, which was before the world was.
(George Fox, 1657, in *QF&P* 2.35)

From the beginning, and for most of its history, the focus of
the unprogrammed wing of the Religious Society of Friends
has been on the inner journey, and an unmediated relationship
with God. Doing without churches and music, stripping away
outward manifestations, rituals, ornamentation and symbols,
enables Quakers to focus on the essential. Replacing a separate
and paid priesthood with "the priesthood of all believers" gives
all Quakers responsibility for their own faith and organisation. In
doing without specific sacraments, it proclaims the sacred nature
of the whole of life. In rejecting prescribed prayer, it emphasises
the importance of speaking only from the heart, from personal
experience. And of listening in the silence.

Meeting for Worship is at the heart of the Quaker way and,
as its name implies, it is not something you can do on your own.
People used to a meditative practice from other religions often
find it attractive but it's important to understand that there is a
distinction. Although held in stillness, and mostly in silence, it
is not solitary meditation but a meeting, a communal activity.

It's hard to describe a Quaker Meeting for Worship. Easy
enough to describe the mechanics –such as they are. We sit
facing each other, usually in a circle. We meet in equality, with
no one taking charge. The meeting begins when the first person
enters the room, and ends when two people who have been
previously appointed shake hands. Then all present shake hands
with their neighbour. In that hour in between we still ourselves,

waiting, listening for guidance. Waiting on God. We may call to our attention those who are absent, sick or recently bereaved or deceased. If someone is moved to speak, when they are clear that what is on their heart is for the meeting and not just for them individually, anyone may stand and speak – this is known as spoken ministry.

Those are the bare bones. But how it feels, what happens in that silence, is wonderfully resistant to generalisation. We can't say what the experience of a Meeting for Worship will be, for it is unpredictable, different each time. Nor can we say how it has been for another. Each person will experience it differently, although on occasion over the post-meeting tea and coffee, we may agree that the meeting had been profound. But, perhaps unfortunately, it's not something that we generally talk about.

And it doesn't always "work" – for whatever reason (usually our own state of mind), we are unable to reach into the potential richness of the experience. I think many of us imagine that others in the room are in a state of receptive emptiness or contemplative bliss. Even if I feel that nothing is happening in the silence, I have to trust that nothing, that emptiness, and be aware that it has its own quality and potential; that it might give rise to an awareness later, or in someone else.

In my experience the self-consciousness, monkey mind or the shopping list gets in the way for a while, and then, maybe half way through, maybe just before the end, it all falls away, and I am left in a calm still connectedness. We have different ways of preparing, of emptying, opening ourselves. Some concentrate on their breathing, on stilling their body, some focus on a few words, but my sense is that reaching a state of receptiveness isn't anything I do – it seems to come from grace or the collective consciousness. I have to let go of trying.

We may arrive grumpy, preoccupied or anxious. At the end of an hour, having put aside those preoccupations for a while, we have reached a different place. In some indefinable way, we are changed. We have been re-energised. And because we know from experience that this can happen, we keep coming.

Meeting is a place where we, with all our differences, including differences of belief, meet. Young and old, newly convinced or a Quaker from birth, attending for the first or the five hundredth time – each individual has an equally important part to play. There is no training, no dogma; we just need to come with a willingness to join with others in stilling ourselves. *Advices & Queries*, sometimes jocularly referred to as the Quaker maintenance manual, is a little booklet that does not instruct us but offers advice and questions. Number 12 reminds us that all present share responsibility for the meeting, whether vocally or in silence. We meet in acceptance, trust, and common purpose: that of listening to the still small voice within us, and to each other.

Here are three accounts of the experience of a Meeting for Worship. First, in one of Chris Goodchild's delightful meditations:

> Here, in the silence, you experience a profound sense of oneness within yourself and with others. It is as though you step off the stage and drama of life and into a very different dimension altogether.
>
> This temporary stepping off the stage of the world and into the cool stillness of meeting for worship has a timeless quality all of its own. For it is here that you put aside your identity as a father, teacher, writer ... and simply drift without the "oars" of methods or creeds upon an ocean that carries you to the divine within. (51)

And two from a little book called *Twelve Quakers and Worship*:

> I wait
> I still myself

I am often encountered
I am always changed
(Quaker Quest, 25)

As the meeting gathers, I believe that a subtle energy begins to work among us. That of God in each of us is meeting the Divine.
(*ibid.*, 26).

The Quaker way is not a Sunday-morning-only religion but one that absorbs the whole of our lives. Our Meetings for Worship can be held wherever "two or three are gathered together in my name" (Mt 20:18). A sitting room, the bedside of a dying person, outside an arms fair, in a seventeenth-century meeting house, or in a rented room above a shop: all places are sacred. London Quakers used to hold a monthly Meeting at Speakers Corner in Hyde Park. Those who know it will know that it is a place where people come to evangelise and shout about their beliefs; there is much ranting and heckling. To hold a still centre in such a place is a rare and powerful experience.

And we can meet at any time. My own Meeting has three meetings a week: Sunday morning, Tuesday lunch-time and Wednesday evening – appropriate times for a central London group. But Quaker worship is not limited to our weekly meetings; it is central to all that we do in community. A still place is held before meals and before engaging in any activity. Indeed, our decision-making procedure is a Meeting for Worship for Business: a gathering not just heralded by worship but rooted in it; the entire process held in a worshipful manner. We are bidden to arrive with an open heart and mind, ready to listen to the Spirit and to the opinion of others. No arguing, no voting; contributions made from a deep place.

It is not surprising that such an all-encompassing practice has an impact on individual lives, many of us finding the need for that still interiority creeping into more of our domestic and working lives, and having an impact on the manner of our being, living and doing. The need to pause, collect ourselves, go within, to feel that spacious consciousness, a connection to all that is. I have given up on listening to the radio first thing, finding an hour or so of silence in the early morning an essential base for the rest of my day. And as I devote more time to reflection and contemplation, that in turn feeds into the depth of my worship. The process is circular.

Sitting in silence is not easy. There's an innate unwillingness to face it. Like a writer faced with a blank page, most people will do anything, find a multitude of activities, rather than stop, still themselves, "waste time with God". When I shed my distractions, I find I have to allow myself to pass through a boredom threshold, to allow myself to be "bored" in order to attain another state. When an introductory programme for those interested in the Quaker way was started, people said that the suggested inclusion of a half-hour Meeting Worship was unrealistic. "People won't manage it. Half an hour is too long." But, in the event, newcomers warmed to it, and some of those Meetings are among the most profound that I have experienced. It needs no knowledge, no previous experience, for the power to be felt.

So where does this experience lead us? What effect does it have on our lives?

Chapter 3

Community

Our life is love, and peace, and tenderness; and bearing one with another, and forgiving one another, and not laying accusations one against another; but praying one for another, and helping one another up with a tender hand.
(Isaac Penington, 1667, in *QF&P* 10.01)

Religion implies community: literally the word means "a tying together". Rabbi Jonathan Sacks says that "a community is where they know your name and where they miss you when you are not there ... society with a human face" (*To Heal a Fractured World*. London: Continuum, 2005, p. 54).

An equally true, if less comfortable, definition was given by the Quaker Parker J. Palmer in 1977:

In a true community we will not choose our companions, for our choices are so often limited by self-serving motives. Instead, our companions will be given to us by grace. Often they will be persons who will upset our settled view of self and world. In fact, we might define true community as the place where the person you least want to live with always lives!
(*QF&P* 10.19)

Any of us can worship alone, but in joining with a specific religious group, we are expressing a need for community – something that is at the heart of liberal religion.

* * *

When I had been attending a Quaker meeting for about six months, our meeting ran a weekend away. I remember my disdain at the theme of the weekend: "Belonging? I've never wanted to belong. Don't believe in it." Although I had and have good friends, I'd never seen myself as belonging to a group. In fact, I'd always felt a bit of an outsider. "Ah," said a friend wisely, "but have you ever met anyone who thought they were an 'insider'?"

By the end of a weekend of sleeping under the same roof as about thirty others, eating together, talking, walking and worshipping, I sat on the Sunday morning with my eyes closed, mentally going around the circle of Friends. I realised I knew everyone in the room. A powerful sense of belonging swept over me. I realised not only that I did belong, but that I had always wanted to. As is so often the case, I had denied what I most desired.

So, what is this Quaker community? Our local community is called a meeting. Although it can be confusing that our religious practice is also called a meeting, it actually emphasises the importance of community in our Quaker practice. Meeting is who we are and what we do.

The Religious Society of Friends of Truth was one of several non-conformist Christian groups that emerged in a period of turmoil in the 1650s, after the English Civil War. So, are Quakers Christian? It's a common question. The roots of our Quaker society are indeed Christian, but even the earliest Quakers recognised a commonality with other faiths.

The humble, meek, merciful, just, pious and devout souls are everywhere of one religion; and when death has taken off the mask they will know one another, though the divers liveries they wear here makes them strangers.
(William Penn in 1693, *QF&P* 27.01)

So, an expression which we often use is that Quakers are "rooted in Christianity and open to new Light". In recent years, as we have become more exposed to other faiths, the "new Light" has become a much broader spectrum. Many Quakers would call themselves Christian (though their definitions might vary); many would not. As we experience a dynamic Spirit in our individual faith journeys, so, as a collective, our sense of community changes. Until forty years or so ago, most Quakers would think of themselves as Christian to some degree; then in the late 1970s there developed a more universalist strand with the formation of the Quaker Universalist Group in the UK, and the Quaker Universalist Fellowship in the US. Now, questions are raised not only about our adherence to Jesus, but to any kind of theism.

We have to be careful that different understandings of language and belief don't obstruct the commonality of our practice. Belief can divide; faith unites. And faith is whole-hearted. As a friend said, you cannot have a bit of faith any more than you can be a little bit pregnant. You either are or you are not; you either have it or you do not. Having lived without faith for many years, I know the difference. We may not know or be able to speak about the nature of what we have faith in, but our not knowing *what* may co-exist with a firm knowledge *that*!

Quakers have a broad, complex and changing spectrum of belief, reflected in the fact that our book of discipline, *Quaker Faith & Practice (QF&P)*, an anthology of writings from the earliest days of Quakers in the seventeenth century to the present day, is updated every generation. As I write, a new edition is being considered, to reflect the changes that have taken place in the last twenty years or so. A belief in continuing revelation is a key aspect of our faith.

Recognising the riches that the practices and understandings of other faiths can bring, Quakers are happy to embrace people who are also Muslims, Buddhists, Jews, from any other major faith, or none. There are a number of attenders at British Quaker meetings who call themselves Quanglicans. A plurality of adherence is not seen as a threat. Many people come to Quakers from other faiths and retain an affectionate loyalty for their former faith home. They are surprised, and relieved, to discover that there is no expectation that in coming to Quakers they have to cut off those ties. As we know in other aspects of our lives, we can have allegiance to more than one thing. Belonging is complex.

But as Ben Pink Dandelion says, the community is key.

Always we need to see our worshipping community as our central focus and resource which supports all else, rather than see Meeting as the optional add-on to a personal spiritual life, if we are to avoid the destructive singularities of individualism.

In meeting with others on a regular basis, we not only find a rhythm in our own spiritual life but a rich experience which is an important part of our Quaker lives and identity. At its best, Meeting for Worship is more than the sum of the individuals taking part and on occasion can bring a powerful sense of unity.

We call such an experience a "gathered meeting".

In such a meeting, we may have a sense of the collective experience, a sense in the silence or sometimes expressed by someone who feels moved to share something with the rest of the meeting. It is surprising how often someone else's ministry may speak what has been on our mind or heart. It's something that might be crudely referred to as telepathy, but it is at a level well beyond party tricks. I remember one occasion when a Friend in my meeting who was over 100 at the time, and very deaf, called me over at the end of the meeting.

"I didn't hear a word that you said," said she, "but what I was thinking was" – and proceeded to express in her own way what had been the content of my ministry!

It is clear from such experiences that this is a collective

practice, something we can only do together, and that sometimes our experience of it merges. Thomas Kelly asks:

> What is the ground and foundation of the gathered meeting? In the last analysis, it is, I am convinced, the Real Presence of God.
> (*QF&P* 2.40)

Arguably this is what makes the Quaker experience unique: it is a *corporate* mysticism. As a former Catholic Quaker said, his former experience had felt solitary – in the presence of others but not part of a communal experience, not, as with Quakers, embodied in the group.

And community is about mutual support, very often at an individual level, as members of the meeting listen at times of trouble, visit in times of sickness or bereavement, uphold each other in prayer or, in a favourite Quaker phrase "hold" someone "in the Light". As a community without a separate priesthood, we all take responsibility for caring for each other, though we do have people – called overseers – appointed to pay special attention to the pastoral needs of the meeting. Sometimes the support is in a less obvious, less visible, way. I remember at a troubled time feeling rather resentfully unsupported by the meeting. Yes, individuals were being kind but I felt that, somehow, and probably unrealistically, the meeting itself ought to be there for me. And then it came to me that it is in the silence of Meeting for Worship that the support, the love, comes. By putting the pain or trouble out there – usually without speaking – there often comes a response, a tender understanding and affirmation. There might also come a different perspective, a different and sometimes challenging perspective on our own behaviour. By opening ourselves to the Light, we have to accept that it might shed its rays on our darkness and, as the first of our *A&Qs* says, in so doing, it "brings us to new life".

I like to think of Meeting for Worship as a triangle of the self, the Divine and the others in the room. And it is that dynamic that we take out into the world. For Meeting for Worship is not just for the polishing of our individual souls, not just "sitting on the cushion", but a collective waiting, a listening for guidance for how we are to be in the world. We sit there in stillness, mostly in silence, but it isn't a passive state. Inspiration may come directly to our inner voice, or through other people, and our actions reflect that.

Chapter 4

Service

*True godliness don't turn men out of the world but enables them to
live better in it and excites their endeavours to mend it.*
(Penn, *QF&P* 23.02)

We all have to find ways of supporting ourselves and our families.
Not everyone can find employment in something that they find
rewarding or a job that fulfils them, and many have to make
compromises in order to survive. Our life's work, if we find it,
may be something quite different from our job. and it may be only
late in life, if ever, that we discover what it is that we are called
to do. As unique human beings, we each have a unique vocation,
a contribution that only we can make. That may or may not be
something that earns money. If we are lucky, our job and our life's
work may coincide for at least a part of our life.

When faith found me (and, yes, it was that way round) I had
been working in publishing for nearly thirty years, latterly as an
independent literary agent. I was already feeling at odds with the
world I worked in. I had loved it, and now I didn't. The celebrity
culture, the bottom-line mentality, made me uncomfortable.
What I was doing no longer met my needs but, with no idea of
what else I might do, I stayed put. It was only the advent of faith
that enabled me to sell my business without any idea of what the
future might bring. For someone who had always planned the
next step with an eye to the CV, it was a transformative and very
freeing moment. Why had it taken me so long to understand that
this was the way to run my life?

Soon after I came to Quakers, I attended the annual meeting
of British Quakers. And I found myself on my feet, ministering
to a hall of nearly a thousand Quakers. Shaking with nerves, and

maybe quaking with the Spirit, I said, "I've been called. I don't know to what, but I know I must let go of my present life."

I no longer needed to know what I was going to do. I knew that I would be guided to whatever came next. And I was. Within a couple of weeks of the decision I received a phone call, asking me to set up a community centre, an invitation that set me on a completely different way of life. Fortunately, I was financially secure enough to take the risk, and my admiration goes out to those – and I know some – who are not but who do it anyway.

Biblically, love means to serve, and it is in service that we find our mission in the world. To interact with our fellow human beings is to do God's work and of course such work is not peculiar to Quakers. As St James wrote: "What good is it, my Friends, for someone to say he has faith when his actions do nothing to show it?" (James 2:14).

The call to service is fundamental to most faiths. In Christianity, the call is to be among the suffering of the world, the dispossessed. Love is the centre of the Gospel. Christ's second commandment is to love thy neighbour as thyself. And the greatest of "Faith, hope and charity" is charity (love) ... For Christians God is love. In Islam to reduce the disparities between rich and poor is a priority: one of its five pillars is charity. Jains must give to charity anything beyond their own needs. Sufis are expected to have a constructive vocation; and, for Sikhs, Guru Nanak said that "true spiritual life meant the performance of duties in the world, and facing and solving the moral and spiritual problems of mankind". (Kavanagh, 150–51)

And so, we come to the word "practical". Why might Quakers be called practical? Not in terms of their ability at DIY – I imagine that we have no more or less of that than others. I for instance am pretty impractical in that sense though there is no doubt that many others are gifted with such skills as to make them of service as wardens of meeting houses, or on premises committees. No, I think the term is used more in the sense of a grounded common sense, in seeing a problem and finding solutions. In getting things done. As the Quaker quoted at the beginning of the book said, "*There is something gloriously no-nonsense about almost all the Quakers I know.*"

Sometimes that practical quality is in dealing with specifics, and in having the patience to see something through. Quaker processes are slow, and maybe that enables us to take the long view. I have always been impressed, for instance, by our United Nations office in Geneva (QUNO), a non-governmental organisation which has been named as one of the world's hundred most influential actors in armed violence reduction, where a group might work on the same issue for years until some progress is made. In the 1970s and '80s, QUNO worked to raise public awareness about the issue of child soldiers, its causes and consequences, and to develop international standards to prohibit the military recruitment and use in combat of people under 18 years of age. This prohibition is now included in the Geneva Conventions on War and the Convention on the Rights of the Child. In taking the specific aim of ridding the world of child soldiers, QUNO has nibbled away at the war machine.

The organisation was also one of the pioneers in gaining international attention for internally displaced persons. "Through perseverance," they say on their website, "we have helped to change attitudes, create new understandings, and develop new standards."

In England, Quaker Social Action, the award-winning independent charity, has been addressing the problems of poverty in the East End of London for some 150 years. Their projects are specific – financial literacy, collecting unwanted furniture and selling them on to those who can't afford more than a nominal amount; providing practical support for people struggling with funeral costs; housing young adult carers. These are very focused projects and solutions, some of which they export to other organisations in other parts of the UK.

For a small organisation – there are currently about 20,000 Quakers in Britain and 35,000 in the unprogrammed tradition (Friends General Conference) in the US – Quakers have had a significant impact of social welfare: in the fight against slavery, in prison reform, and in being instrumental in the founding of such organisations as Amnesty International, Oxfam and Greenpeace.

Quakers played a major role in the abolition movement against slavery in both the United Kingdom and in the US. They were among the first whites to denounce slavery in the American colonies and Europe, and the Society of Friends became the first organisation to take a collective stand against both slavery and the slave trade, later spearheading the international and ecumenical campaigns.

In 1947 Quakers were awarded the Nobel Peace Prize. Here is an excerpt from the award-giving speech:

The Nobel Committee of the Norwegian Parliament has awarded this year's Peace Prize to the Quakers, represented by their two great relief organizations, the Friends Service Council in London and the American Friends Service Committee in Philadelphia.

For it is not in the extent of their work or in its practical form that the Quakers have given most to the people they have met. It is in the spirit in which this work is performed. "We weren't sent out to make converts", a young Quaker says: "we've come out for a definite purpose, to build up in a spirit of love what has been destroyed in a spirit of hatred. We're not missionaries. We can't tell if even one person will be converted to Quakerism. Things like that don't happen in a hurry. When our work is finished it doesn't mean that our influence dies with it. We have not come out to show the world how wonderful we are. No, the thing that seems most important is the fact that while the world is waging a war in the name of Christ, we can bind up the wounds of war in the name of Christ. Religion means very little until it is translated into positive action."

One of the people to receive the award on behalf of Quakers was no other than Rufus Jones. Not only imbued with mysticism from an early age, he was also a social activist and co-founder of the American Service Committee. A prime exemplar, one might say, of a "practical mystic".

The Religious Society of Friends as a group had first been nominated for the Nobel prize as early as 1912, just eleven years after the award was founded. It was nominated again in 1923, 1924 and 1936. On each occasion the nominations were influenced by Quaker relief work with the victims of war and famine.

The extraordinary achievements of Quakers over the years can be daunting. I remember mentioning to a South African lawyer that I had just become a Quaker. "Oh, Quakers," he said, "I'll never forget what they did in the anti-Apartheid movement." It's hard to live up to such a history, and it's important to remember that we are called to different kinds of service: both in form or approach and in the area of concern.

In the area of peace-making, some will be called to direct action, non-violent protest against arms sales or nuclear submarines, breaking the law where they feel they are upholding the laws of a higher power, and risking imprisonment; some will be tireless in their campaigning; some will go into schools to talk against militarisation; some will hold peace vigils and pray for peace in all parts of the world; some will engage in community or family mediation; some will train themselves and others to become more peaceful in their everyday lives and in their hearts. Peace, it is said, begins with us, and is a process – often a very slow one.

Quakers have become known at their United Nations Office, in Northern Ireland, and in other parts of the world for creating quiet diplomacy, enabling warring factions or diplomats from different sides to get together discreetly, and, without the glare of the world's media, attempt to find common ground. "I pin my hopes", said Rufus Jones in 1920, "to quiet processes and small circles, in which vital and transforming events take place" (*QF&P* 24.56).

Peace is perhaps the area of work for which Quakers are best known, but some people are drawn to work with marginalised people, such as people sleeping rough, seeking asylum or in prison. Others will be drawn to homemaking, work with children or elderly people, or to work on dementia, death and dying, mental health, community or interfaith relations, or any number of other areas – each in their different way. What we find ourselves working in is not the result of external pressure or from a sense of duty, but because of a movement of the heart. Poverty and injustice are so widespread that to make an impact we have to find the concern that moves us. "The place God calls you to", says Frederick Buechner, "is where your deep gladness and the deep hunger of the world meet" (*Wishful Thinking: A Seeker's ABC*). And finding the place of deep gladness is where discernment comes in, as we'll see in Chapter 7.

It may be surprising to learn that not only have Quakers been involved in social action and philanthropy but that in earlier days they had an exceptional track record in banking and running businesses, including their pioneering sense of responsibility to their employees. Barred by law from much of public life, they had to find opportunities in other areas, and their probity in business dealings attracted large numbers of customers. Quakers were people you could trust. In more recent times, with more opportunities open to them, fewer Quakers have been involved in financial affairs, except in trying to establish alternative, more egalitarian ways of running businesses.

In all this, it is important to remember the importance of the work behind the scenes, faithfulness in what Gerald Littleboy calls "inconspicuous service". "For some", he says, "it is right to give their whole lives explicitly to concrete forms of service, but for most their service will lie 'in the sheer quality of the soul displayed in ordinary occupations'" (QF&P 23.66). Faithfulness in the small things of life can be the hardest task. Bringing probity and compassion to our chosen occupation – whether as homemaker, plumber, barber or entrepreneur – is not easy, nor is trying to change the values from within a corporate structure. It's a mistake to think that "action" has to be some grand act of social engagement – changing the world. Everything we do, including transforming ourselves, is a form of action. Mother Teresa famously said that there is no such thing as a small piece of work: once you give it to God, it becomes infinite.

As Quaker Deborah Haines wrote in 1978,

I think I have wasted a great deal of my life waiting to be called to some great mission which would change the world. I have looked for important social movements. I have wanted to make a big and important contribution to the causes I believe in. I think I have been too ready to reject the genuine leadings I have been given as being matters of little consequence. It has taken me a long time to learn that obedience means doing what we are called to do even if it seems pointless or unimportant or even silly ... We need to develop our own unique social witness, in obedience to God. We need to listen to the gentle whispers which will tell us how we can bring our lives into greater harmony with heaven.
(QF&P 23.52)

This is not to deny the place of prophets and visionaries. There has been no lack of such Quakers over the centuries. Although they may not always be the easiest people to live with, without them

33

little would be achieved. In order to work towards creating the Kingdom of God (or Commonwealth of the Spirit) on earth, there has to be some vision of what that might be.

What makes action specifically Quaker? Jonathan Dale wrote that it is "a different and deeper way of responding to the needs of the world, in that it relates our current human concern to the ultimate source of all concern" (21). But that difference might be applied to all faiths. Action with or without faith is different in quality, both in terms of where it comes from and in the manner of working. I think the Quaker contribution might be something more specific.

The Quaker way requires us to take responsibility. It is very much a do-it-yourself religion – or rather, as we have seen, a do-it-together one. As an organisation of the priesthood of all believers, we all need to take responsibility for our own faith, our organisation and funding, and our religious community. I believe that that attitude extends to taking responsibility for the world at large. We do not rely on experts, politicians or others. There are no other hands but ours. But, even more importantly, it's because of the nature of the core of the Quaker Way: the relation between the manner of our collective worship and how we act in the world.

From the beginning the emphasis among Quakers has been not on creed but on a way of life. George Fox, generally considered to be the founder of the Religious Society of Friends, asked his fellow-Quakers to:

> be patterns, be examples in all countries, places, islands, nations, wherever you come, that your carriage and life may preach among all sorts of people, and to them; then you will come to walk cheerfully over the world, answering that of God in every one. (A&Q, 42)

Quakers are often quoted as believing that "there is that of God in everyone", but what George Fox actually said was "Walk cheerfully" (which at that time bore the meaning of purposefully) "over the world *answering* that of God in everyone". Fox took it for granted that there was that of God in each human being: what he was asking for was an active response.

In the following poem W.B. Yeats describes not only a mystic experience in his everyday life, but the loving response it evokes in him.

My fiftieth year had come and gone,
I sat, a solitary man,
In a crowded London shop,
An open book and empty cup
On the marble table-top.
While on the shop and street I gazed
My body of a sudden blazed;
And twenty minutes more or less
It seemed, so great my happiness,
That I was blessèd and could bless.

That of God in the self, answering that of God in the other.

Love finds expression in action. As Evelyn Underhill says: "The use and meaning of the spiritual senses are strictly practical." A person accesses Reality not, as she says "in order that he may gaze upon it, but in order that he might react to it, learn to live in, with, and for it" (1991: 104).

How is this done? What makes something specifically Quaker is as much in the manner of working as in the work itself. The Quaker Social Action website makes the point:

What we do matters, but how we do it matters too – our focus is on the person not the problem. We believe that people in poverty are the real poverty experts.

We enable people on low incomes in east London and

across the UK to seek solutions to the issues affecting their lives.

To do this we listen and respond to the needs of the community by running practical, sustainable and collaborative projects.

We share our work with others when it is clear that it has the potential to bring benefits to communities outside of our own.

What I learnt when I first was asked to do some voluntary work was that it was about being alongside, about recognising the mutuality of what we were doing – that it was at least as much benefit to me as it was to the person without a home, a country, or in prison. And that we can be transformed by the encounter. Even when approaching something with an unwilling and begrudging attitude, our mood and our understanding can be changed. I realised that the people I was working with did not somehow fall into separate categories of being: "the homeless", "asylum seekers". And that it could have been me. That there is no such thing as "the other". These understandings made a profound and lasting difference to my perceptions, and to my preconceptions.

Watching how other volunteers worked, I saw how different this was from the common perception of "do-goodery". Of course, Quakers don't have a monopoly in good practice, but our testimony to equality is central to the way we work. In starting a mobile library for homeless people, for instance, we were providing a service where we were all on an equal footing: we were not giving a hand-out that might be seen as patronising or humiliating, but having a conversation about books, providing a loans service that was set up to be as much as possible like any library for the rest of the community.

It's important not to duplicate what others are doing, but to discern what can be our specific contribution. And to work with others. Quakers are particularly good at providing a platform for action. In 2018, in preparation for the mass march against the visit of the American president, Donald Trump, to the UK, they held a Meeting for Worship at Friends House in London, which was attended by many non-Quakers: both clergy from other denominations and those without faith.

And in our own lives, what is our responsibility? There's a balance between our own preparation and practice on the one hand, and the work of the Spirit. Between our own responsibility and what is given to us without us having earned it in any way. Everything is rooted in worship. Our collective experience tells us that it matters how we set up the practical arrangements, providing the time and space for worship to happen. And that we prepare ourselves, coming to Meeting and to the work we do "with hearts and minds prepared". But, even in unexpected or adverse circumstances, we can fall into worship.

Grace can overwhelm us.

Chapter 5

Faith into action

There is an experience of the Eternal breaking into time, which transforms all life into a miracle of faith and action. Unspeakable, profound, and full of glory as an inward experience, it is the root of concern for all creation, the true ground of social endeavour. This inward Life and the outward Concern are truly one whole, and, were it possible, ought to be described simultaneously. But linear sequence and succession of words is our inevitable lot and compels us to treat separately what is not separate: first, the Eternal Now and the Temporal Now and, second, the Nature and Ground of Social Concern.
(Kelly, 89)

What is the relation between our faith experience and our action: what we do, how we are, in the world? It is not a simple causal or sequential relationship. That we are changed, that is certain – we become part of a larger consciousness, aware of our connection with other human beings and other creatures – and it will probably affect *how* we are in the world.

When I came to Quakers, I was not looking for a community, but I found one – and a very empowering one. Brought up in a society that believed that poverty and injustice are just too big for us to make a difference, that there's nothing we can do, I was now meeting people who *were* making a difference, in small, local ways, maybe – volunteering for this, campaigning for that – but it was enough to liberate me to believe that I too might do something. I was electrified, released from the dead hand of hopelessness. I was being given permission – and the opportunity. Networking is a strong quality of most Quakers. I found that whatever I asked brought the response: "I know someone who will know," and an introduction.

Suddenly, with my quest for a home for my spiritual seeking came an impulse to help make the world a better place and the opportunity to recover my youthful idealism. The first thing that I was asked to do was to co-ordinate the tea-runs for people sleeping on the streets that several London Quaker meetings were running. I became a trustee of Quaker Homeless Action, and one of the best memories of those early days in the late '90s was of a group of people sitting round a table and, as necessary tasks arose, several immediately volunteering: "Oh, I'll do that, I'll do that." My oldest Quaker friend, and one of my dearest, is someone I met at QHA: there's no doubt that doing something together creates a lasting bond.

So, where does this impulse for service come from? From the earliest days of Quakers, the vision has been of building the Kingdom of God on earth, to bring into reality the values that are both implicit in and a direct result of our worship. As Rufus Jones says, the vision that we may be given in worship is not an end in itself. "More important than the vision", he says, "is the obedience to the vision." And that obedience leads to action. "His mission on earth is to be a fellow worker with God" (1940: 89, 90).

This impulse has a lot to do with the nature of Meeting for Worship, which is not a passive experience, but an expectant waiting for guidance. What we experience in that hour may make itself felt immediately or may slowly trickle down into our consciousness, and the impact felt days or weeks later. On rare occasions we may feel, understand, something quite specific during Meeting – and it's not always what we want to hear.

"Really?" we say, aghast. "Oh, no, don't ask me that!"

A friend talks of a major change in her life that she took very seriously because the need for it came to her in Meeting for Worship.

And sometimes there is a shift in our understanding,

sometimes we have "a leading" that moves us out in the world in a different way. Our changed selves will have an impact on the people, around us, on the world. And we may be led to start something, a challenge that is not always welcome!

So how do we get from here to there? In his lecture on "Living our Faith Daily: the practice of testimony" given to Ireland Yearly Meeting in July 2018, Ben Pink Dandelion explores the nature of that mysterious connection:

> We cannot be touched by the divine and stay as we were ... this kind of encounter is essentially and necessarily transforming. We are spiritually transformed in order to go out into the world to help transform it. Our daily life is our testimony to our experience of spiritual encounter.

What we are called to is not an externally imposed duty but an inner imperative. Nor is it a causal or sequential matter, as in "I have faith, and therefore I act". Faith and action feed each other. Jonathan Dale writes of his own experience:

> I know that faith can be deepened – even refound – in action. I know that in "doing" I have experienced states of "being" that cannot be discovered in any other way. (51)

And he quotes Amanda Wooley:

> My activism draws on spiritual roots to give it nourishment, grounding and discernment. Meanwhile, through activism, my spirituality comes alive and my inner life is fed with learning and insight.
> (*ibid.*, 50)

Integrating this sense of unity into our lives is not easy. Gordon Matthews calls for a more deeply rooted experience:

We need both a deeper spirituality and a more outspoken witness. If our spirituality can reach the depths of authentic prayer, our lives will become an authentic witness for justice, peace and the integrity of creation, a witness which becomes the context for our prayer. Out of the depths of authentic prayer comes a longing for peace and a passion for justice. And our response to violence and injustice is to pray more deeply, because only God can show us the way out of the mess that the world is in. And only God gives us the strength to follow that Way.

(*QF&P* 23.10)

The importance of the relationship between our faith and how we are in the world cannot be overstated. The Quaker way is experiential; it is a lived faith. As our *Advices & Queries* have it, "Let your life speak" (27). We do not have a creed; no one joining a Quaker meeting is asked to sign up to anything. But the way we try to live – with integrity, being true to our authentic self, trying to do what love requires of us – is at the heart of our commonality. This way is expressed by what we call testimony. As Ben Pink Dandelion says, "Our transformed and transforming life is testimony to our experience of spiritual encounter." Or, more expansively, as Harvey Gillman describes it:

The word "testimony" is used by Quakers to describe a witness to the living truth within the human heart as it is acted out in everyday life. It is not a form of words, but a mode of life based on the realisation that there is that of God in everybody, that all human beings are equal, that all life is interconnected ... These testimonies reflect the corporate beliefs of the Society, however much individual Quakers may interpret them differently according to their own light. They are not optional extras, but fruits that grow from the very tree of faith.

(*QF&P* 23.12)

This concept of testimony or testimonies is a key aspect of the Quaker way. To call testimonies "values" is to secularise what is a spirit-based connection. As Jonathan Dale says,

> The especial importance of the testimonies in the practice of Quaker faith is that they form unbreakable bonds between spiritual insight and social action. This unbreakable bond preserves us from the dualisms which oppose faith and action, personal salvation and the building of the kingdom of God (20).
>
> In all that we say and do we intend to hold firm to our core testimony to the sacramental nature of each aspect of our lives in so far as we sense in it God's loving purpose. So, in the crucial economic and political areas of our common life we must practise spiritual discernment. And then act.
>
> (From a paper produced by the Recovering our Social Testimonies group in 1997, quoted in Dale, 11)

Like some other Quakers, I prefer to talk of testimony in the singular. To list them, as we often do, as testimonies to peace, equality, simplicity and truth, and an evolving one to the Earth, is to simplify them and to suggest their separation, when in fact they are interconnected. And it also suggests that they are set in stone, whereas, as Gillman says, they are not a form of words, but an evolving way of life. One of the reasons that Quakers do not have a creed is that we believe that the Spirit is dynamic, and we may understand something differently tomorrow from how we perceived it yesterday.

The expression of our testimonies has evolved. In the early days of Quakers, simplicity, for instance, was exemplified by the wearing of plain dress. Now our focus on what matters may take the form of a resistance to the consumer culture, and what blocks us from God may be over-busyness, an excessive attachment to material possessions or the demands of an over-active ego. In the early days, expressions of the testimony to equality included the refusal by male Quakers to remove their hats, and an insistence on addressing everyone with the familiar "thou", both of which were seen as an insult to those considered worthy of deference. Now, for instance, our focus may be more on the importance of same-sex marriage, or the involvement of children in decision-making processes.

There was also a testimony against the arts: dance and singing were forbidden until comparatively recently. Viewing such activities now as an important part of the beauty of God's creation and our expression of Divine creativity, we find it hard to understand why they should ever have been banned from Quaker life.

It is important to realise that testimony is both corporate and individual and to understand the distinction. Jonathan Dale feels that a corporate understanding and unity may be found in the general direction of a testimony, whereas difference in individual interpretation may be expressed in the precise path. Being faithful in all we do, in all the small activities of our world, living in a way that is true to our faith – a committed, dedicated life as an instrument of the Divine – that is a hugely challenging path. In all our daily doings we fall short. We know only too well that we don't live up to our aspirations. *Advices & Queries* serves to remind us of our commitment and to challenge any tendency to complacency or hypocrisy. One of the most useful advices is the last sentence of number 17: "Think it possible that you may be mistaken."

How are we to live our faith daily? We are to be priests one to another, continually coming forward to each other, washing each other's feet: if that motion of love is the heart of our practice of testimony, the living of our daily faith, our inhabitation of being Quaker in the world (our testimony), shall come all the more easily.

(Dandelion)

Chapter 6

Discernment

Spiritual discernment lies at the heart of Quaker spirituality and practice. It's grounded in the central Quaker conviction of the availability in each person of the experience and guidance of God ... It is that infallible intuitive gift we use in attempting to discriminate the course to which we are personally led by God in a given situation, from our other impulses and from the generalized judgments of conscience.

To undertake to live a discerned life, to endeavour daily to be attuned to authentic movements of the Spirit leading us into greater fullness of life, is a strenuous undertaking.
(Loring, 3,15)

How do we know what it is that we are meant to do? Early Quakers, like biblical prophets, often spoke of hearing the voice of God telling them to take a certain course of action. Nowadays, I think that is a rare occurrence, although it did in fact once happen to me.

I was walking along the road when I heard, or rather felt, a big voice vibrating within me say "Preach". Preach? I wondered. Quakers don't preach. But over the years I have come to realise that, uncomfortable though I am with the word, perhaps what I have been called to since then – the writing, public speaking, teaching – could be called preaching.

But in general, Quakers tend to be suspicious of the "showy" guidance that is more characteristic of the charismatic Churches. We generally describe our experiences as nudges, prompts, a sense of inner conviction, which may come during Meeting for Worship or, often unprompted, at other times. I find that inspiration comes often when I am walking by water, in woods or in fields. The rhythm of the walking, the tranquillity and presence of the natural world, enable a creative movement in our heart and mind. Most of all being away from the computer and other distractions.

> How do we stay in that space of an accompanied life, listening to divine advice and instruction? How do we know when we are being faithful and not just following our own imagination? Well, we might look for the signs of the fruit of the Spirit (Gal. 5:22), or feel something as "simply right": perhaps everything just slots into place and energy flows freely.
> (Dandelion)

In Matthew (7:20) we also hear: "By their fruits shall ye know them." The fruits can be in increased quality of "being" – awareness, awakening – or increased doing. The best of all worlds is doing with increased being. That, I believe, is the true fulfilment of our human potential as spiritual beings. Manifesting the spiritual in the world by what we are, what we do. And how we do it. As the passage in Galatians identifies it, in "love, joy, peace, longsuffering, gentleness, goodness, faith".

Margery Post Abbott has developed what she calls a system of "inner markers" of God's presence. These include: "times of spontaneous prayer, a sense of overflowing joy, a deep sureness about action or words ... A word or phrase that jumps at me out of a page, or a book that begs to be read" (28).

When we are at a time of transition, or faced with a knotty problem, we often have to wait for clarity. I used to pride myself on being decisive, and would sort out my problems very much on my own. I have had to learn to stop, and wait. That the way forward is not just about my rational mind, or pushing to make things happen, but all sorts of other factors, not least other people. For an impatient species (and particularly for this individual!) waiting is hard.

I've come to realise that waiting is at the core of the spiritual life. The title of the French mystic Simone Weil's most famous book is *Waiting on God*. It is also how we describe the experience of a Quaker Meeting for Worship: in stillness and mostly in silence, it's a collective listening for guidance, a collective waiting on the Presence, waiting on God. And so it is in the rest of our lives. In enabling time and space for the Spirit to enter, we might find a completely unexpected way forward. Frequent obstacles and rejections may show us that we are on the wrong path; affirmations may show us that we are on the right one. And, in my experience, such guidance very often comes through other people. A phone call can open up a new and exciting opportunity, which we would never have thought of on our own. And through a series of seeming coincidences – synchronicities – that move can be confirmed.

I have come to rely on synchronicity. In the late 1990s I was fortunate enough to get a Churchill Fellowship to study the practice of microcredit – lending small amounts of money to (mostly) women living in poverty, to enable them to start their own businesses. I started such a programme in the East End of London and when I returned from a year's travel in 2002, I was keen to apply my understanding of microcredit to other countries. One day, I picked up a free newspaper and found a page on Madagascar – a country I knew nothing of, not even its location (a very large island off the East coast of Africa). In the corner of the page was an advertisement for a charity asking for volunteers to go to Madagascar. One of the things they were hoping to work on was "sustainable income generation". Sounds like microcredit, I thought, and rang them. Indeed, they said, that was the sort of thing they were looking for. In the event I did not feel suited to that organisation, but as I explored the possibility, the name of Madagascar came at me from every direction: "Oh, you must meet so and so, both her sons married Malagasy women," "Oh, Friends (Quakers) are very involved in Madagascar" and, sorting out the Quaker Meeting library, I came across *100 years of Friends' work in Madagascar*. Eventually, I heard that a home for destitute girls near the capital was already training the older girls in skills to help them make the transition from the home into the outside world, and was keen to start a microcredit programme. And so, in March 2004, I went.

"The realisation of a discerning life", says Ben Pink Dandelion,

is about the asking and the finding of the holy sense of the what, the when, and the how. It is about living in the space of humble unknowing with a readiness to learn. It is about, as it is in our Quaker meetings for worship for business, of setting self aside. It is about having our feet in the stream of the living waters of Spirit. For me, every moment matters, every decision is to be offered up to ideally be blown through, winnowed, with the winds of the holy spirit, for the wheat to settle, the truth to be found. Indeed the decision itself may be less important than being in the space from which the decision can be made.

Unguided by dogma or liturgy, we as Quakers are more reliant on our own ability to discern the way forward, which has its own dangers. American Quaker Parker Palmer acknowledges that "the conviction that every human being has direct inward access to God" needs to be balanced by "the equally strong conviction that we need a community to sort and sift what we think we are hearing from within ... Not every voice from within is the voice of God" (quoted in Dawes, 29).

For this reason, the responsibility for spiritual nurture is shared by the members of the meeting. Discernment is not just an individual matter, but something for the community as a whole. In discerning the way forward, one resource open to an individual Quaker is the Meeting for Clearness, in which five or six Quakers are invited to listen to an individual who has an issue they wish to sort out. In a carefully structured process, those invited do not give advice, but listen carefully and ask questions in order to enable the Friend to find clarity – which may come at that time, or sometime later. The whole process depends on trust and confidentiality, and is held in a prayerful manner.

If an individual has a powerful sense of a leading of the Spirit towards a certain course of action that might involve the meeting as a whole – what in Quaker circles is called a "Concern" – there is a well-trodden path for testing it, taking the issue first to the local business meeting then, if accepted, it is forwarded to wider Quaker groups. If it seems to have potential for national application, it might then be forwarded to the national representative executive, which might in turn refer it to a specialist committee for guidance. Quaker processes are slow.

> In larger issues the discernment process often does not produce a full and clear plan of action ... In my own experience, once I have accepted the call, there is plenty of work for my intelligence to do, and great need of advice and support from others ... If I am doing what I would call God's work, I need to trust that I am "in good hands" and to respond sensitively and flexibly to what unfolds.
> (Lampen, 59)

Decisions that affect the whole meeting, or a larger body of Quakers, are made at what are called business meetings – a rather off-putting name for our worshipful decision-making process. These meetings, whether at a local meeting level, for a committee, or for a larger body, are quite unlike the processes of decision-making in the rest of society. They have an agenda, but otherwise are conducted like Meetings for Worship. We are urged to come with an open heart and mind and a willingness to listen and be sensitive to other points of view. There is no voting or argument, and those present are expected to speak only once on a particular topic (although in practice that is waived if someone comes from a position of special knowledge).

Contributions are from the heart and out of the silence. Discernment is mediated by the clerk, who attempts to ascertain not the consensus, but the sense of the Meeting, indeed, the will of God through the Meeting, from both spoken and silent contributions. If there is no sense of unity, the matter is deferred or a small group may be set up to look into it in detail. When the meeting agrees that the time is appropriate, the clerk reads out a draft minute, which is then and there amended, accepted and owned by those present.

In a wider society that emphasises individuality, taking part in or agreeing with the conclusions of corporate discernment is not always easy. Quaker decision-making is often mocked for its slowness, but it is a powerful and sensitive method, offering space for conclusions which may not have been in anyone's mind before the meeting began. It is something, I believe, that Quakers have to offer the world and has, indeed, been adopted in non-Quaker contexts.

Chapter 7

Finding the balance

What is given in the vision, on the mountain, is the raw material. Everyday life is the factory, where one tries to make sense of it. Perhaps the moment when one is "taken out of oneself" is the moment of eternity experienced in the here and now; the isolated self is reincorporated into the larger Self. This may be expressed both as a losing of self or as a finding of Self; a death or a rebirth.

The mystical path is a process into the world, not a series of wonderful, extraordinary experiences leading out of it ... The mystical path is not one of escapism. It is one of commitment.
(Gillman, 14, 15)

Traditionally, Christian monastic life is divided into time spent in prayer, reading of the scriptures and physical labour.

The spiritual life in the world also consists of a series of balances: between the life within and the outside world, between responsibilities which might include earning a living, juggling care for children or elderly relatives and an array of other commitments and our own spiritual practice. The balances of inner experience and outward witness; being passive to God and active to the world; between withdrawal and engagement, being and doing.

In the seventeenth century, George Fox said: "The Lord taught me to act faithfully in two ways – inwardly to God and outwardly to all."

In Christianity the story of Martha and Mary is familiar: the one called to the way of service; the other to contemplation. Many people seem to harbour a sense of guilt. If engaged in the world, they worry about not being very "spiritual"; if leading an interior, prayerful life, they are concerned that they are not "doing their bit". The truth is that no one is either one or the other, but somewhere on a spectrum between the two – there is a variety of spiritual expression that exemplifies the richness of possibility inherent in lives devoted to God. An individual inclination or a phase of life may be tilted more towards outward action or contemplation, and it will vary at different times of life, but we can work towards a way that is more integrated, more in balance.

How do we do it? Finding the balance on a daily or yearly basis is a common preoccupation. Few people feel that they get it right. Mostly we're too busy, assaulted by noise and information. The practicalities of being in the world – our commitments to our Meeting and to the outside world – are pressing; we sometimes find it hard to breathe. It's not easy but, even at the busiest times of life, it is possible to pause. A practice like this can be such a small matter: a pause for gratitude before a meal; indeed, a pause before embarking on any activity, to make its intentionality clear; a pause during the day to take stock, centre ourselves. In that pause, like the moment between one out-breath and the breathing in, or between a wave receding and the swell of the next, is a space of another dimension. Even if it is not feasible to take chunks of time away from our responsibilities, it is possible to establish a rhythm, take time in the week or in the day to stop for a little, maybe finding a time of day to devote to prayer, yoga, reading, meditation or other practice that enables a more spacious consciousness. Or to find opportunities for unplanned reflection – waiting for a bus, or going up the stairs.

I must say that I know more Quakers who tend to the practical, who find it hard to stop, hard to say no to service on a committee or voluntary work at the local food bank, whose only pause is for a weekly (or occasional) Meeting. But even then, the *manner* of what they do will be changed. Their way of life, their very being, will be affected by their Quaker faith and practice.

And those who feel they are not doing enough? What are

they expecting? What do we mean by action? All of life is action. Everything we do. And it is not just what we do but how we do it – in love and mutuality – and how we are. We are each unique. When we surrender to God's will, the call comes to us as an individual because of who we are, with all our gifts and faults. Listening to what love requires of us will allow us to maintain a balance.

A life of prayerful service is not an either/or; the ideal is to hold the two in balance. Thomas Kelly, who died in his early forties in 1941, the year of publication of his wonderful study of and guide to the mystic way, *A Testament of Devotion*, was much influenced by Rufus Jones, with whom he studied at Haverford College in 1915. He too served on the American Service Committee; he too was a practical mystic. He writes of the simultaneity of this way of life:

> There is a way of ordering our mental life on more than one level at once. On one level we may be thinking, discussing, seeing calculating, meeting all the demands of external affairs. But deep within, behind the scenes, at a profounder level, we may also be in prayer and adoration, song and worship and a gentle receptiveness to divine breathings. (35)

Elsewhere, Kelly refers to the seventeenth-century French lay brother, Brother Lawrence, whose book, *The Practice of the Presence of God*, is a slim volume of letters and conversations describing just that: a way of life in which everything is done for the glory of God; an active title for an active expression of our faith. Brother Lawrence spent years washing up in the monastery kitchen, every moment consecrated, in the present and in the Presence. For such people there is no distinction between worship and daily life: all are one. Simple, and the hardest thing in the world.

When I first came to Quakers, some twenty years ago, I jumped in with both feet. It was as if I had been given a spiritual kick up the backside. "It's taken you long enough; now get on with it!" I plunged into a pendulum kind of life, swinging between intense activity and periods of remote solitude. Time in conflict resolution, with homeless people, in prisons, and setting up microcredit projects in the UK and various African countries was interspersed with days spent in isolated little huts in various parts of the country. Now, though I still struggle to get the balance right, I'm grateful to have settled into something a little more equable. Sometimes, when we find ourselves immersed in busyness, it's helpful to be reminded: "Between actions, pause and remember who you are." In that pause we can collect, gather ourselves, find again that spacious consciousness from which authentic action comes.

> The truth is that no life is either completely active or completely contemplative; we are all somewhere on the spectrum between the two extremes. "Love", says Carlos Carretto, "is the synthesis of contemplation and action," and we are all called to different kinds of love in action. "I have known the satisfaction of unrestrained action," he says, "and the joy of contemplative life in the dazzling peace of the desert, and I repeat again St Augustine's words: 'Love and do as you will'". St Teresa is of the same mind: "What does it matter if we serve in one way or another."
> (Kavanagh, 146–7)

It could be said that to make any kind of distinction is a false dichotomy. Prayer is action; faith is inherent in our engagement in the world. We express our faith in how we live our lives, how we are in the world, as patterns and examples. The Quaker way is a holistic one: faith consumes our lives.

Despite the claim that contemplation and action are one, there are still conflicting views of their relationship. Thomas

Merton and Thich Nhat Hanh, Trappist and Buddhist monks respectively, say that contemplation is only half the job – that the object of years of practice is to make one more fit for action in the world; that the movement of the Spirit in us is to be enacted among other people. The other viewpoint is that the *vita activa* must precede the *vita contemplativa*, that action is preparation for contemplation, that indeed active periods of life are the dry times, the fallow periods from which contemplation will develop. The truth would seem to be that the two are indissolubly connected: each feeds the other (*ibid.*).

Chapter 8

Practical mystics

It is a vital discovery of the divine Life revealing itself here and now in and through a group of persons who are bent on transmitting that Life. It is mysticism not of solitude and self-seeking; it is practical mysticism of life and action.
(Jones, 1927: 170)

There is no inconsistency between a mystical life and a practical life. The more truly mystical a person is, the greater the probability that he will be effectively practical. (ibid., 202)

It was the mystical that pulled me into Quakers: that was what I found spoke to the deepest part of me. It was not surprising that it was the universalist element to which I was drawn. As my faith went deeper within me, I realised with delight that I was treading on ground that was familiar to my parents. My father, initially an Anglican, converted to Catholicism when I was five; my mother, initially a non-practising Jew, found the Kabbalah, the mystic end of Judaism, in her fifties. For all of us, the mystical was what mattered; we were reading the same books; our different labels didn't matter. As Roswitha Jarman writes: "As a mystic I am linked to mystics of all faith communities with whom I share the longing for understanding and living this unity" (94).

It's a paradox that an experience that can lift one on to a realm beyond the everyday world so often drives us to engage with that world and changes the nature of that engagement. I had no notion that Quaker worship would also pull me into engagement with the world – no idea that it would be the very practice that resulted in that engagement. No idea that anything could bring together my mystical inclinations and my youthful idealism.

As one former Catholic said to me, "I wouldn't be interested in a mysticism that was not practical. It's about *being* the change, being the Presence, living it."

And as the Dutch priest, Henri Nouwen, wrote:

> True contemplatives ... are *not* those who withdrew from the world to save their own soul but the ones who enter into the centre of the world and pray from there (144–5). Mysticism is the opposite of withdrawal from the world. Intimate union with God leads to the most creative involvement in the contemporary world.
>
> (*ibid.*, 177)

Activism

Even the most renowned of mystics, throughout the centuries and across cultures, have found in the most profound contemplation a need to respond to God's love by reflecting it back to others; a need to respond to the iniquities of the age: whether church corruption or social and political violence and injustice. Most have managed to speak out from within the structures of the established church, though often ignored, criticised, persecuted or even expelled for doing so.

In the twelfth and thirteenth centuries (long before the word mystic came into being) there was an extraordinary flowering of women contemplatives in Europe who were also activists, reflecting, perhaps the lack of opportunities for women at that time for positions of power in the established Church. These included the multi-talented Hildegarde of Bingen (1098–1179), German Benedictine abbess, philosopher, artist and composer, who denounced the evils of the state and the church, and Catherine of Siena (1342–80), whose mystic experiences dated from early childhood and who in her teens insisted on living the life of a reclusive anchoress, later emerged to work in the community, teach and engage in politics before her early death.

In the twentieth century, we find, among other activist mystics Simone Weil, French mystic, philosopher and political activist, whose commitment to the sufferings of the poorest led to her depriving herself alongside them, dying eventually of malnutrition at the age of 44, and Thomas Merton, Trappist monk and Thich Nhat Hanh, Buddhist monk, united in their opposition to the Vietnam war.

Conversely, some of those known primarily for what they do in the world were moved by their faith. Talking of the heroic lives of Joan of Arc and Florence Nightingale, Underhill says that:

> they both acted under mystical compulsion ... Their intensely practical energies were the flowers of a contemplative life ... It is ... the function of a practical mysticism to increase, not diminish, the total efficiency, the wisdom and steadfastness, of those who try to practise it.
>
> (1991: xv)

Among Quakers, prominent figures are often known more for their social works than their mystic tendencies, but from the diaries of the nineteenth-century prison reformer Elizabeth Fry, for example, it is clear how her work was rooted in prayer. In quieter, less heroic lives, the same is true. Roswitha Jarman is a contemporary Quaker. She is a peace activist, winning a peace award in 2005 for her work in Northern Caucasus. She has also taught extensively on the medieval mystic, Meister Eckhart and is the author of *Breakthrough to Unity: The Quaker way held within the mystic traditions*.

Many individual Quakers today still live out their faith maybe in less visible but nonetheless remarkable ways. Some blog about their experiences, such as Craig Barnett, the co-founder of the City of Sanctuary movement, who took his family to live in Zimbabwe when he was appointed director of Hlekweni Friends Training Centre in Matabeleland. He writes about the faith that underpins his life and work in http://transitionquaker.blogspot. com/ "Hay Quaker" blogs about how he lives out his commitment to simplicity and sustainability in http://hayquaker1.blogspot. com/.

But maybe today our practical mysticism is exemplified more by collective action – such as sessions at our annual Meetings for Worship for Business when it was decided to support same-sex marriage, or divest from fossil fuels; in programmes such as Turning the Tide, which trains people in non-violent action. The first question in a workshop they ran recently on spirituality and activism was "What moves you to act?" Some witness is overtly part of the mystic reality of our worship practice: peace vigils, regular Meetings for Worship outside Faslane Nuclear Submarine Base; Meetings for Worship and silent, candle-lit vigils in solidarity with victims of the arms trade outside the biennial Defence and Security Equipment International arms fair (DSEI) held in east London. As Sam Walton, Peace and Disarmament programme manager for Quakers in Britain, said: "Britain surely cannot promote peace and democracy, and London cannot be a city of peace, if it is where repression and torture begin and if it is where the seeds of war are sown." Quakers involved in any form of direct action, such as nonviolence resistance or marching for peace, root themselves, centre themselves in worship. The one stems from the other.

Mysticism

Books on mysticism tend to take a historical approach, and mentions of Quakers nearly always refer to the early years of the movement, and to individuals from that time such as George Fox, William Penn and, in the next generation, the theologian Robert Barclay. It would be easy to assume that the Religious Society of Friends was an interesting seventeenth-century movement.

William James, writing in 1902 about the seventeenth century, gives a fulsome example:

The Quaker religion which [George Fox] founded is something which it is impossible to overpraise. In a day of shams, it was a religion of veracity rooted in spiritual inwardness, and a return to something more like the original gospel truth than men had ever known in England. So far as our Christian sects today are evolving into liberality, they are simply reverting in essence to the position which Fox and the early Quakers so long ago assumed. (7)

In the eighteenth and nineteenth centuries the Quaker mystical tradition was continued by John Woolman, whose story I will tell later, and other writers whom we sadly ignore today, such as Caroline Fox and Caroline Stephen. More recent mentions of Quakers have tended to concentrate on their social activities. There is little said that affirms the mystic quality of the Quaker way in itself, or makes it clear that it is alive and kicking in the present day. Surprisingly, there is no mention of Quakers in Happold's study and anthology of mystic writing, and even in Lucinda Vardey's wonderfully wide-ranging compendium of contemporary spiritual writings, *God in all Worlds*, there is not a Quaker to be seen. It also has to be said that among modern Quakers there is little talk of mysticism. Maybe we have been failing to write of the mystic quality of our faith, or remiss in getting it to the attention of the wider public. In his splendid anthology of the Quaker way, *The Spirit of the Quakers*, Geoffrey Durham has gone some way towards putting that right and, of course, the various versions of *Quaker Faith & Practice* round the world are a treasure chest of writings about all aspects of Quaker life and faith over the last 350 years.

Maybe the invisibility of Quaker mysticism is also because the nature of it is a) collective and b) practical, making it inseparable from service and the community. Faith in action.

Maud Grainger, the Faith in Action tutor at Woodbrooke Quaker study centre, is unequivocal about the connection, applying it specifically to our Quaker meetings:

An active meeting is one that is gathered in God. It has to be active because that's what God is calling us to as a community. An "active" meeting that is not gathered in God is not Quaker but an activist group. If it says it is gathered in God and is not active it is not truly gathered.

Jonathan Dale applies these views to individual lives:

We need the illumination of social testimony to lead us into spiritual wholeness, to a place where all things – from our perusal of our bank statements to our trip to the filling station – are held in our hearts in the Light of God's loving truth. (63)

Few mystics give accounts of their experience. By its very nature an ineffable experience is hard to describe. That is even more true of a corporate experience such as a Quaker Meeting for Worship, which may be distinguished only by the depth of the silence or the connectedness of the spoken ministry. Occasionally an individual will have a powerful experience within that communal practice. Many years ago, I remember seeing, as it were, a golden band round the waists of each of us, linking us all together. But I don't think I spoke of it.

Our reluctance to speak of our experiences may also be because of a fear of seeming to think of ourselves as "special", a fear of "showing off". A very British, and maybe a very Quaker, fear! And the practicality of Quakers is expressed in subtle ways, in the quality of their lives, of everyday decisions, expressions of love and compassion.

We have considered so far, the definition of "practical" as denoting "inclined to action" or "engaged in practice, working etc." – both of which are indeed definitions from the Oxford English Dictionary. But the first definition given, dating from the sixteenth century is "of, pertaining or relating to practice". Quakers, as we have seen, are indeed practical in the sense of the first two definitions, but so much more so, uniquely, perhaps, in *the manner of their practice*. It is not only in the outcomes of practice but in the practice itself, in Meeting for Worship, that Quakers might claim to be practical mystics. Like the title of Brother Lawrence's book, it might be said to be the practice of the presence of God.

The following definition of mystics was given in a dictionary of theology written in 1856:

> Under this name some comprehend all those who profess to know that they are inwardly taught by God. The system of the mystics proceeded upon the known doctrine of the Platonic school ... that the divine nature was diffused through all human souls ... They lay little or no stress on the outward ceremonies or ordinances of religion, but dwell chiefly upon the inward operations of the mind.
>
> (Quoted in Robinson, 50)

This might have been written about Quakers. But for Brother Lawrence, the practice was in his everyday life, doing everything for the love of God.

> He said that he was always ruled by love, with no other interest, without concerning himself about whether he would be lost or saved. But having taken as the end of all actions, to do them all for the love of God, he was well satisfied therewith. He was happy, he said, to pick up a straw from the ground for the love of God, seeking him alone, purely, and nothing else, not even his gifts. (5)
>
> He was even more at one with God in his common activities than when he turned from them for the formal activities of retreat, from which he would return to common life only with much dryness. (11)

That is our challenge. It is all very well to affirm that the whole of life is sacred. In rejecting the need for special rituals, special times and places, there is a danger that nothing in fact will be sacred. Unless we pay attention, unless we face every moment with committed intention, there is a danger that the sacred will be lost.

A Quaker friend responded to the title of this book with some scepticism and, in a splendidly down-to-earth (I would say practical) way, emailed me to say:

> The mystic vision is a way of understanding human existence which may bubble up through anyone open to receive it, and is shaped by any framework or dismissed as too much cheese for supper or the onset of madness. The mystic vision may lead to sitting in stillness at home alone or with others in a Meeting for Worship, sitting meditating in a cave up a mountain, holding others in love, or going on a demonstration and getting arrested. I personally cannot single out any of these expressions and call it more "practical" than any of the others.

I hope I have answered her concerns, demonstrating both that the mystic vision is not confined to Quakers, and that the practicalities of those who experience that vision may be expressed in many ways.

Maybe we feel that "mystic" is too big a word for us individually, but the Quaker way is without doubt a mystical one. I might conclude that not all Quakers are mystics, but that we will all, in some way and to some degree, be touched by the mystical, sometimes held by it and even, in some, be taken up in its all-encompassing embrace.

So far from being a contradiction in terms, the practical is the lifeblood of mysticism: we are not being asked to detach ourselves from our humanness, to float off into some kind of numinous ethereal space. Even in our mysticism, we are relating to others. The practical is both the natural outcome of the mystic experience and intrinsic to the experience itself. There is no division between being and doing.

Practical mystics are still with us, not least among Quakers.

Practical Mystic: John Woolman, 1720–1772

John Woolman is an outstanding example of a Quaker who lived out his faith, and one of the best-known and best-loved figures in Quaker history. He is remarkable, not only for what he did but for the gentle manner of his doing. The panel of the Quaker tapestry about him says "His beliefs went beyond religion to the guidance of the Absolute Truth".

Woolman was born and brought up near Philadelphia in New Jersey. Raised a Quaker, he was the eldest son of a large family, and reported that he had been subject to mystical experiences from an early age.

He kept a journal for much of his life. Such was his humility, he rewrote it several times to try to delete as many mentions of the word "I" as he could! Among Quakers, he is most famous for three aspects of his life and witness: his work against slavery, his approach to the American Indians, and his identification with the suffering and dispossessed, including animals. Unusually for his day, Woolman expressed a love of animals from an early age.

Slavery

Surprisingly, in the 1750s, despite a testimony against owning slaves in the States, there were still Quakers who did so. Working on a personal level, Woolman tried to persuade slave-owners to change their ways, and often succeeded. While working as a tailor, he also did conveyancing and wrote wills for people. He records in his journal that, on one occasion,

> a neighbour ... desired me to write his will: I took notes, and, amongst other things, he told me to which of his children he gave his young negro: I considered the pain and distress he was in, and knew not how it would end, so I wrote his will, save only that part concerning his slave, and carrying it to his bedside, read it to him, and then told him in a friendly way, that I could not write any instruments by which my fellow-creatures were made slaves, without bringing trouble on my own mind. I let him know that I charged nothing for what I had done, and desired to be excused from doing the other part in the way he proposed. Then we had a serious conference on the subject, and at length, he agreeing to set her free, I finished his will.
> (*QF&P* 20.46)

Although his method was by quiet and individual friendly persuasion, Woolman's work was influential. Frederick Tolles, a chronicler of the period, considered that:

> more than any other single influence, it was Woolman's clear and steady voice that woke the conscience of the Quakers and ultimately, through them, of the Western world to the moral evil of slavery (quoted in Sox, 58).

Indians

In the previous generation, William Penn (the Quaker founder of the State of Pennsylvania) had led the way in treating Indians as equals but after his death, things changed. Despite recent violent interactions, Woolman felt moved to approach the Indians again. In a famous passage, he explained his motivation:

Love was the first motion, and then a concern arose to spend some time with the Indians, that I might feel and understand their life, and the Spirit they live in, if haply I might receive some instruction from them, or they be in any degree helped forward by my following the leadings of Truth amongst them. (QF&P 27.02)

Woolman's suggestion that he might have something to learn from the Indians was quite revolutionary at a time when Indians were regarded as sub-human, dangerous, and, even if approached non-violently, it would be with the intention of conversion.

* * *

In 1772, Woolman undertook the longest journey of his life – and the last – to England. Unlike the other passengers, despite ill-health, he insisted on travelling in the cramped and unhealthy conditions of steerage, alongside the seamen. "I was now desirous to embrace every opportunity of being inwardly acquainted with the hardship and difficulties of my fellow creatures" (quoted in Sox, 95).

In England, Woolman travelled extensively among Quakers. At first, English Quakers were taken aback by his strange appearance: wearing only undyed cloth, mostly as part of his protest against the use of goods provided by slave labour. He refused to travel by stage coach, because of the suffering of the horses and the ill treatment of the boys who drove them.

These decisions were expressions of the guiding morality of his life: his identification with those who were disadvantaged or suffering. Whether slaves, Indians, seamen, coachmen or animals, Woolman wanted to be alongside them. Like the French Simone Weil some two hundred years later, he put his health at risk in order to identify with those who had least.

He never returned to the US, catching smallpox and dying in

York in 1772.

The subtitle of David Sox's biography of John Woolman is "Quintessential Quaker".

And so he was.

David Sox, the biographer of Woolman, was born in North Carolina and active in the Civil Rights movement with Martin Luther King. He was ordained an Episcopalian minister then moved to London where he taught at the American school, was active as an Anglican minister, and became a member of my Quaker meeting in London. Like Woolman before him, he cared deeply about the way animals were treated, and said that, since moving to England, he was focusing the same passion that had led him to work with Luther King on working for animals. After some forty years in England, he went back to the States where he died in 2016.

I was much moved by David's account of leaving flowers at Woolman's grave in York. He says:

Perhaps it was a silly gesture, but I remembered the words of John Greenleaf Whittier in 1871: "I have been awed and solemnized by the presence of a serene and beautiful spirit redeemed of the Lord from all selfishness, and I have been made thankful for the ability to recognise and the disposition to love him."

And so do I.

Further Reading

Advices & Queries (A&Q). London: The Yearly Meeting of the Religious Society of Friends (Quakers) in Britain, 2010

Quaker Faith & Practice (QF&P). London: The Yearly Meeting of the Religious Society of Friends (Quakers) in Britain, 1995

Dale, Jonathan, *Faith in Action*. London: Quaker Home Service, 2000

Dandelion: https://quakersireland.files.wordpress.com/2018/07/ben-pink-dandelions-public-lecture-iym-2018.pdf

Dawes, Joycelin, *Discernment and Inner Knowing*. FeedARead.com, 2017

Durham, Geoffrey, *The Spirit of the Quakers*. Newhaven and London: Yale University Press, 2010

Fox, Matthew, *Original Blessing*. Santa Fe: Bear & Co, 1983

Gillman, Harvey, *Wrestling with the Stranger*. Work in progress.

Happold, F.C., *Mysticism: a study and an anthology*. Harmondsworth: Penguin, 1970

James, William, *The Varieties of Religious Experience*. Harmondsworth: Penguin, 1985

Jarman, Roswitha, "Mysticism and the Quaker Way" in *the Friends Quarterly*, July 2006

Jones, Rufus, *The Flowering of Mysticism*. London: New York, 1940

—*New Studies in Mystical Religion*. London: Macmillan, 1927

Kavanagh, Jennifer, *The World is our Cloister*. Ropley, Hants: O Books, 2007

Kelly, Thomas, *A Testament of Devotion*. New York: Harper & Bros, 1941

Lampen, John, *Quaker Roots and Branches*. Alresford, Hants: Christian Alternative, 2018

Lawrence, Brother, *The Practice of the Presence of God*. Rockport, MA: Oneworld, 1993

Loring, Patricia, *Spiritual Discernment*. Wallingford, PA: Pendle Hill, 1992

McGinn, Bernard (ed.), *The Essential Writings of Christian Mysticism*. New York: Random House, 2006

Quaker Quest, *Twelve Quakers and Worship*. London: Quaker Quest, 2004

Nouwen, Henri, *The Genesee Diary*. London: Darton, Longman and Todd, 1995

Post Abbott, Margery, *Quaker Views of Mysticism*. Walllingford: Pendle Hill, 2004

Robinson, *Paths between Head and Heart*. Winchester: O Books, 2018

https://criticalconversation.files.wordpress.com/2014/02/essential-writings-of-dorothee-soelle.pdf

Sox, David, *John Woolman: Quintessential Quaker*. York: Sessions, 1999

Underhill, Evelyn, *Mysticism*. Oxford: Oneworld, 1993

—*Practical Mysticism*. Guildford: Eagle, 1991

Walters, Kerry (ed.), *Rufus Jones, Essential Writings*. NY: Orbis Books, 2001

Also in this series

Quaker Quicks - Practical Mystics
Quaker Faith in Action Jennifer Kavanagh
ISBN: 978-1-78904-279-5

Quaker Quicks - Hearing the Light
The core of Quaker theology Rhiannon Grant
ISBN: 978-1-78904-504-8

Quaker Quicks - In STEP with Quaker Testimony
Simplicity, Truth, Equality and Peace - inspired by Margaret Fell's
writings
Joanna Godfrey Wood
ISBN: 978-1-78904-577-2

Quaker Quicks - Telling the Truth About God
Quaker approaches to theology
Rhiannon Grant
ISBN: 978-1-78904-081-4

Quaker Quicks - Money and Soul
Quaker Faith and Practice and the Economy
Pamela Haines
ISBN: 978-1-78904-089-0

Quaker Quicks - Hope and Witness in Dangerous Times
Lessons from the Quakers On Blending Faith, Daily Life, and Activism
J. Brent Bill
ISBN: 978-1-78904-619-9

Quaker Quicks - In Search of Stillness
Using a simple meditation to find inner peace
Joanna Godfrey Wood
ISBN: 978-1-78904-707-3

CHRISTIAN
ALTERNATIVE

THE NEW OPEN SPACES

Throughout the two thousand years of Christian tradition there
have been, and still are, groups and individuals that exist in
the margins and upon the edge of faith. But in Christianity's
contrapuntal history it has often been these outcasts and
pioneers that have forged contemporary orthodoxy out
of former radicalism as belief evolves to engage with and
encompass the ever-changing social and scientific realities. Real
faith lies not in the comfortable certainties of the Orthodox,
but somewhere in a half-glimpsed hinterland on the dirt track
to Emmaus, where the Death of God meets the Resurrection,
where the supernatural Christ meets the historical Jesus,
and where the revolution liberates both the oppressed and
the oppressors.

Welcome to Christian Alternative... a space at the edge where
the light shines through.
If you have enjoyed this book, why not tell other readers by
posting a review on your preferred book site.
Recent bestsellers from Christian Alternative are:

Bread Not Stones
The Autobiography of An Eventful Life
Una Kroll
The spiritual autobiography of a truly remarkable woman
and a history of the struggle for ordination in the Church of
England.
Paperback: 978-1-78279-804-0 ebook: 978-1-78279-805-7

The Quaker Way
A Rediscovery
Rex Ambler
Although fairly well known, Quakerism is not well understood.
The purpose of this book is to explain how Quakerism works as
a spiritual practice.
Paperback: 978-1-78099-657-8 ebook: 978-1-78099-658-5

Blue Sky God
The Evolution of Science and Christianity
Don MacGregor
Quantum consciousness, morphic fields and blue-sky
thinking about God and Jesus the Christ.
Paperback: 978-1-84694-937-1 ebook: 978-1-84694-938-8

Celtic Wheel of the Year
Tess Ward
An original and inspiring selection of prayers combining
Christian and Celtic Pagan traditions, and interweaving their
calendars into a single pattern of prayer for every morning
and night of the year.
Paperback: 978-1-90504-795-6

Christian Atheist
Belonging without Believing
Brian Mountford
Christian Atheists don't believe in God but miss him: especially the transcendent beauty of his music, language, ethics, and community.
Paperback: 978-1-84694-439-0 ebook: 978-1-84694-929-6

Compassion Or Apocalypse?
A Comprehensible Guide to the Thoughts of René Girard
James Warren
How René Girard changes the way we think about God and the Bible, and its relevance for our apocalypse-threatened world.
Paperback: 978-1-78279-073-0 ebook: 978-1-78279-072-3

Diary Of A Gay Priest
The Tightrope Walker
Rev. Dr. Malcolm Johnson
Full of anecdotes and amusing stories, but the Church is still a dangerous place for a gay priest.
Paperback: 978-1-78279-002-0 ebook: 978-1-78099-999-9

Do You Need God?
Exploring Different Paths to Spirituality Even For Atheists
Rory J.Q. Barnes
An unbiased guide to the building blocks of spiritual belief.
Paperback: 978-1-78279-380-9 ebook: 978-1-78279-379-3

Readers of ebooks can buy or view any of these bestsellers by clicking on the live link in the title. Most titles are published in paperback and as an ebook. Paperbacks are available in traditional bookshops. Both print and ebook formats are available online.

Find more titles and sign up to our readers' newsletter at
http://www.johnhuntpublishing.com/christianity
Follow us on Facebook at
https://www.facebook.com/ChristianAlternative